FROM
BAGHDAD ON THE TIGRIS TO BAGHDAD ON THE SUBWAY

NOTE YET CHOSEN

WALID A. HINDO

ARCHWAY
PUBLISHING

Archway Publishing books may be ordered through booksellers or by contacting:

Archway Publishing
1663 Liberty Drive
Bloomington, IN 47403
www.archwaypublishing.com
1 (888) 242-5904

Because of the dynamic nature of the Internet, any web addresses or
links contained in this book may have changed since publication and
may no longer be valid. The views expressed in this work are solely those
of the author and do not necessarily reflect the views of the publisher,
and the publisher hereby disclaims any responsibility for them.

Any people depicted in stock imagery provided by Thinkstock are
models, and such images are being used for illustrative purposes only.
Certain stock imagery © Thinkstock.

ISBN: 978-1-4808-3402-6 (sc)
ISBN: 978-1-4808-3403-3 (e)

Library of Congress Control Number: 2016910874

Print information available on the last page.

Archway Publishing rev. date: 09/08/2016

CONTENTS

Dedicated to my good friends, the Sorority of the Bibs, who received and encouraged me to make it available for the American public. Namely, Mrs. Leona Orhenstein, Mrs. Isabel Schechter, and Mrs. Yetta Hirschenbein

Special thanks to my daughter Dr. Heather Hindo M.D. for the encouragement, support and reviewed parts of the book.

ACKNOWLEDGEMENTS

I would like to thank Mr. Maneli Reihani- Masouleh who was the first contents editor. Miss Sarah Gwen, editor who handled all of the submissions. And to the organization of Archway Publishing company. I would also like to thank Mr. Alfredo Martin Orias and Ms.Iva Dawis for hours of typing, correcting, and zeal in the research of names and dates.

ANNOUNCEMENT

A great care was been taken to change the names of people, institutions and dates to cover the identity of the people mentioned in the body of this book. Any resemblance to people living or dead is purely accidental.

PROLOGUE

The plane which I took was rather of a wide bodied plane from London's Heathrow Airport to New York's JFK Airport. The people were also big and of wide girth. I often heard "Parla Italiana" so I guess they were all Italian immigrants. The reason the plane was full is because that week, all of the U.S. airlines were on a strike and they have left the skies to the united states, from Europe and the Far East were serviced by airlines that do not carry an American flag. I closed my eyes and fall asleep then woke up on the sound of screaming and clapping so when I asked the flight attendant what they were celebrating.

He said "They have just announced that the plane crossed the continental land" this was my first flight ever to any country and I felt relieved that we are flying over land again.

The trip in my country was not without its own problems. The government was changing everyday with the lack of security provided by the Army. I was one of the lucky ones because when I was assigned by the Army through lottery after finishing six months in the Military Reserve College, my commander in the Army Surgical Unit was the youngest colonel. He was also Christian and he had great respect for people who were trained by Jesuits like I was. So when I joined the Military Advance Surgical Group of the first division, I did not have the support of any influential person in Iraq like most of my comrades who each came up highly recommended from high ranking officials of Iraqi Army.

So when I reported to Dr. B Boghossian(1), a commander of the unit, he asked me "Who is your reference?" I said "No one, sir. I have no recommendation"

"How come your father was one of the highest ranking officials in the Army under the Old regime and not give you any recommendations?" he said

I told him "My father offered to assign me somewhere in the South, not in the North where there was actual hostility" I continued "But I preferred to do it on my own"

I and the other four physicians who have just finished training at the Military Reserve College and have been assigned to the first medical advance surgical group, which have been mobilized to go the North from its permanent position as being stationed in the South. After a short ride, we were presented to the commander of division. After our own commander presented us to the Commander of the Division and assigned each of the four newly minted officers, I was the only one whom he did not mention where I would be stationed.

The commander asked him "Boghos, where are you going to put this young man?" and he motion at me

Boghos replied "I am going to keep him with me for a while"

Then after we were dismissed, the commander called Boghos to come back. Then Boghos said to me "Come on, let's go together"

So I followed him to the commander's office and the commander began chiding Boghos and said to him "Boghos, I heard you are favoring the Christians with nice appointments, putting them away from the hostile fire. Is that true?"

"The only one I know that is a Christian is a guy called Kirkour(2) and only Armenians are called by that name but I don't know any Christians from the Hundreds that have been assigned to our units and if you are unhappy with my assignment of the new appoint, because I know he was Christian, I only knew that today. When I asked him what his relation to the General, he told me he was his son" Boghos answered

I had to smile because I knew he had four other Christians working in the Advance Medical Surgical Unit.

This was my first introduction to the corruption of the Army where ethnic, religion, and tribal relationship have more effect on your job selection even to places like Military health. Moving fast forward about two year later, Boghos and I became good friends. One day he was asking about the American ECFMG (Education Council for Foreign Medical Graduates) (3) Exam which became necessary for any graduates of any medical school in the world to take and succeed (by answering 70% of the medical questions correctly) and obtain a grade A or pass in the English exam which was only for understanding and mastering the American-English language. In addition, the student applicant has to get a certification from the dean of the medical school from which he or she is graduating, that in six months, he or she will be finished with all of the requirements for graduation

Dr. Boghossian asked me weather I was preparing to take the ECFMG exam and I told him I took the exam already and passed it. When I was in the final year of medical school, He asked me "Why are you not going to the United States?"

I answered him, though I passed the exam and the requirements, I have not received the official certificate from the ECFMG administration in Philadelphia. Though I did receive an invitation to come to the United States from one of the hospitals in Pennsylvania, Boghos said that the hospital would not have sent me a contract if I have not passed the exam.

So he said "Let me see what I can do to help you get out of this miserable country."

Then Boghos asked me the next day to come to his office and inquired from me weather I do have some relatives outside Iraq. I mentioned to him that my grandfather is a physician and lives in Damascus (4), Syria.

He said "Great, I want you to write me a petition to take a leave of absence from your current post here in the North and to ask to go to Syria because of your grandfather's illness."

My grandfather was really ill so I did not have to lie, but like in all corrupt countries, you had to get your passport from defense department and you have to take your leave of absence from the Ministry of Health. He recommended that I dawn my military clothes when I went down to Capitol. When I went to the Ministry of Health, I found out that my class was going to be discharged from the army service within a month, I hurried back to Irbil (5). When I told Boghos the news of releasing our class from the Military service, he was very happy.

He said to me "I am going to discharge you from you post ten days before the official discharge comes, because you do have a military passport and somebody might notice that you have this kind of document and maybe will able to stop you from leaving the country."

So he supplied me with two letters addressed to whom it may concern, stating that I am still actively enlisted in the army and that I am in an official visit to see my ill grandfather in Damascus. The only obstacle that remained was getting to American Visa which would have been dangerous to show on my passport as designated place as I was to go to Damascus and then presumably come back to Baghdad. As luck would have it, a good friend of mine was working in the American Embassy in Baghdad.

I told her "I do need a visa to be picked up from Damascus." When she asked why I told her I may go from Damascus to Europe before going to the America. So she said that it was not a problem.

The night I took the bus from Baghdad to Damascus, there was still another revolution and the boarders were closed except from buses that are already on the road. However, every town was stopped by, driver of the bus told the armed police about me and I had to show them letters of my Commander and they let me pass. As the bus became close to Jordan (6), the bus driver announce he is not going to Damascus directly but will go through Jordan. I looked at my passport and the only thing recorded was permission to go to Syria, so I told the bus driver about my dilemma and he said he could stop anywhere, I want but he has instructions to go through Jordan. So I did something I have never done since I took my pen and wrote next to Syria "Jordan, Lebanon, Turkey, and United States" (7) and then we reached Damascus in the morning. So after saying hello to my grandparents, I hurried to the American Embassy.

The lady in the front office was polite but very definitive in her voice and demeanor and she took a long time to look at my passport.

Then she said to me, "Doctor, you cannot use this passport to travel to the states." I replied "Why is that?" She said to me "The passport is missing your date of birth and where you were born".

She said to me "I will be very happy to give you your visa if you could just go to the Iraqi embassy which is not too far away from us. I am sure that if everything is ok with your passport, they will be glad to fill it in"

Then she said "I hope to see you before long".

I had no choice but to go to the Iraqi Embassy. There I met a clerk who said to me "I received from Baghdad this morning that there are no passport or visas to be issued to anybody who present themselves to the embassy. In fact there are three planes ready to take anybody who comes in like you asking to add up information to his or her passport"

I was really mad at myself for not noticing the missing information and my eyes got misty, I sat down not knowing what to do and luck strike again in the form of a military attaché (8) that passed by and automatically stood up and saluted him.

He said to me "You look like you are distressed, son. Why don't you come to my office?"

I told him "No, thank you, sir. I am sure you are very busy with the revolution that occurred last night in our country"

But he insisted so I relented and went with him to his office. He asked me what the problem was. I told him that my grandfather was sick when I came to Damascus to see him and that he needs to go to States with me and that the American Embassy needed s verification of my age and that the clerk refused to write it.

He asked me "Do you have official documents that the states your legal age?"

I had to think very hard quickly and remembered that my driver's license was with me, I showed it to him.

He called the clerk and said to him "I want his passport to be completed as requested; he is going to sit down with me here until everything is completed".

About ten minutes later, I was in the American Embassy and the lady had no way but to put the visa inside my passport. I had the perfect passport because it has the stamp of Iraqi Embassy on it. So I went to Syrian Arab Airlines (9) and I ticketed from Damascus to New York without any stops in the way.

I was happily surprised when the plane had the interior design and the plush seats. There were few people in the plane which allowed me look through the window as this was my first flight ever. I could not believe my luck with the recent incident, I was on my way to Valhalla (10), the New York (11) of my dreams. I was fascinated and delighted to see the snow on the mountains and in the flight was filled with soft music and the pilots took pains to show us the structures on the cities below. At Heathrow Airport, I found out where my connection flight as the Italians were jamming the airport terminal, I sat in front seat with white sheets because of the overbooking at Air Italia due to the strike of American flight and complete shutdown. From JFK Airport I took a taxi to Brooklyn where my aunt lived. She was younger than me by 2 years and was so happy to see me that I felt all the jet lag gone. She was married to a student, at the same time secretary of the Syrian Embassy and she just had a baby boy. There was really very little extra space at her place. But I managed to sleep on the couch. One evening she came from her work, she insisted on taking us to a nice restaurant. I felt I would see her again in New York when the contract with the hospital normally put a little money in my pocket. So the next morning I got up early and called the hospital in Central Pennsylvania and told the operator that I do have an appointment as a resident in their hospital. He looked at the list of residents and could not find my name.

Then a doctor came on the phone and said to me, "Doctor you have had an appointment with us about 2years ago and now we are filled"

He said "In that year there was a shortage of physicians but this year, we have a plethora of residents and all the hospitals in the area have been filled, so I cannot help you"

I put down the phone and ended the discussion by saying, "You cannot help me"

Then at dinner that night my aunt said she would make a few phone calls to doctors she knows who are from our country and who may be in position to help me. He was very successful OB/GYN who was working in Yonkers, NY (12). He was very warm and happy to talk to me and said though his hospital has filled their quota of residents and interns for the current year, however, he has heard that neighboring hospital is looking for intern. He asked me to come to St. Joseph the next morning and he will accompany me to the hospital. The next morning I took a train all the way to northern Bronx and then take the bus to Yonkers. It was a small facility compared to other hospitals but the warmth and joy was unusual. I was soon introduced to director of the hospital. He commented on my Mastery of the English and especially the use of idioms.

Then he asked "When can you start?"

I told him "How about today?"

He said "Unfortunately I don't have a magic wand to facilitate your appointment because it is a little bit after twelve and the day is gone. How about tomorrow"

"Fine" I said

He said "Let's go to our country club (13) to have lunch." And asked me about Iraq

I told him unfortunately my country a dark dawn has descended on it with the army having no leader and therefore they are changing governments without the emergence of a leader for who can articulate a program of development. He said he guessed as much just from reading reports in the newspapers and magazines. Then we left in his car back to the hospital.

As we sat down and he said to me "How much was your trip Iraq to New York?"

I had the receipt which was about three hundred English pounds. He asked the secretary to come and escort me to where my living quarters would be. As I came back he gave me a check for five hundred and ten dollars.

I told him "What is this for?"

He answered "It is our custom to pay the cost of intern and residents and certainly your fare was much lower than most of the residents and interns we hired"

So I went back home in Brooklyn and aunt's husband was home and showed him the money.

He said "What did you do, did you steal it from a bank?"

I said "No, this is an incentive"

We had wonderful dinner at one of the most expensive restaurants. My aunt was so happy with me and of course I gave them about three hundred bucks. I was telling them how happy I was and like in the song, New York, New York, "If I can make it there I'll make it anywhere." Then I got a call from my cousin.

And he asked me "Where are you staying?"

I told him I signed a contract with a hospital in New York

He said "No, cancel it, I found you a spot a Henry Ford Hospital"

And he was insistent on my coming to Detroit. Then my brother in law called and also asked me to come to Detroit (14). There were no planes and I had to take the bus from New York to Detroit.

In Detroit, my cousin asked me "What do you think of the killing of JFK (15)?"

So I told him "I don't know much about the killing of JFK but must be a conspiracy (16)"

My cousin started yelling "You are like all Arabs, always thinking about conspiracy how are going to deal with the residents at Henry Ford? Now be careful now to talk about conspiracy because they will kick you out of the hospital"

He yelled at me for about two hours so I went back on bus to New York that night. My cousin came to pick me up to go a cabaret that night, I told him "I'm going back to New York that night because if I stay in Detroit either I will kill my cousin or he will kill me first". The next day I was in New York.

OPTUS 1: THE O. HENRY WARD (17)

I was a resident in surgery. At July of 1968, in New York, the chief of radiology, who was the only one working, noticed me. Approached me and off handedly asked "Have you done an angiogram?"

I said "No sir"

"Would you like to do one?" he quipped

I said "Sure, what do I have to do?"

He said there was a patient who was about to depart, lying, with no identity and picked up by the ambulance from one of the whore houses in the wharf on 50th street. "He was naked like a baby and unconscious. I would like to give you the experience of doing an angiogram"

I was hesitant for a minute and said "What if something goes wrong? I have never done one before"

He said to me "don't be a sissy, nothing will go wrong. I'll be with you and even if something goes wrong, he is a charity case"

So I went to the charity ward. The man appeared in his late sixty, bald and with few red hairs in his eye brows. No signs of rigidity, normal reflexes, no evidence of trauma visible on his front and back. He looked to me as if he is in deep sleep. And had what appeared to me grin of satisfaction. I waved all signs of hesitation on my part because the chief of radiology told me that he is going to the Angiogram and I was the only help, as it was Saturday. I shaved the little hairs that were there. Then being satisfied that the area was aseptic, I covered the body with clean sheets and covered the body with a blanket. I started rolling towards the Angiogram.

When the chief of Radiology came running down the hall, barely catching his breath and yelled at me "Stop, stop"

I saw a whole bunch of people following in.

The chief of Radiology whispered into my ears "Hope you did not nick him while shaving the area"

I nodded "negative"

A lady tall with indeterminate girth asked me "Could I see his face?"

So I pulled the sheet from his face, he still had that smile of satisfaction.

The lady said "It is him" and the rest of the people surrounding her nodded their heads in the affirmative, when the corridor was empty again I asked the chief who is the man.

He said to me he was the Chairman of the board who has been missing for a week.

OPUS 2: THE BE MEDALED SPEAKER

It was early in the morning, attending the meeting of Chairmen of Departments of Radiology (18) this time I was more confident at the beginning of my status as a Chairman, having an Apple Award (19) which voted as the professor of the year by the senior students of graduating class. Quite frankly I was surprised by getting the award for the seventh year in a row.

The elevator door opened and it was loaded. The crowd of medical students were listening to the multicolor be meddled young man who obviously, was an important speaker at the conference. Judging by the multiple ribbons that were attached to his name plate, I heard my name being softly muttered by a few students near me.

As I turned around the multiple ribboned professor asked me "How is the weather in Chicago today?"

I said to him "Okay, I'll tell you once I look it up in the newspaper" to laughter and giggling of those who were surrounding him.

Then the elevator made a stop. I was hurrying out of the elevator as I wanted to get some coffee and Danish. I saw the young professor excusing himself and trying catching pace with me, when he caught up with me.

He said to me "Can I join you for breakfast?"

"Sure, you can! But do I know you from somewhere?" I retorted

He said to me "You should doctor" then showed me a manuscript titled elementary radiology where I was the co-author.

I apologized to him and we had a hearty breakfast.

OPUS 3: IN THE TRADITION OF
BEN CASEY (20)

It was a hot morning in July; I was ready to move downtown from Yonkers. The rotating internship was almost over. Then I got a call to get in the ambulance. The interns at that time were the medics that rode in the ambulance in lieu of the fire men or the current day paramedics. Since the ambulance drivers travel at high speed many of the interns at Yonkers general were reluctant to ride, the administration then decided to pay each intern 15 dollars each ride.

At the site of accident, there was also a large group of people, onlookers, and several bodies on the ground.

I loved such scenes, the police telling the out lookers to get out of the way and make place for the "Doctor" as I moved, somewhat pompously to examine the injured.

There was hush from the crowd, then silence as I said with a loud voice "please do not move the patients as you may do more harm than good"

Then I moved to a patient who looked like he needs some ventilator, there was a middle aged man who was dressed in a fine suite kneeling beside the injured person and doing artificial respiration. So I asked the man to move away from the patient. He did that promptly. I thought I should apologize as I was rude yet he saved the man on the ground, but I could not find him and I rode the ambulance back to younkers.

That afternoon I was ready to visit several hospitals for interviews to land a position of first year resident in surgery. So I decided to go the biggest hospitals as I was sure they will reject me as I was an ECFMG, is not a graduate of an American school of medicine, who are the ones favored the most.

I sat down in the secretary's office then she said you may go in. As I opened the door I thought to myself, this interview will be brief. Then the chairman rose from his chair. I could have collapsed from astonishment. He was the same person I had rudely treated that morning. I guess he saw my jaw dropping as I started to murmur an apology, but he would not allow me to speak.

He looked at my file and said "Congratulations young man, you do not have to wait for a letter of acceptance as I welcome you to our residency program"

Then after a small talk he said "You may leave now"

As I turned to leave he said "Oh a comment about the accident this morning. I simply loved the way you handled the triage, you got balls young man"

OPUS 4: THE RELUCTANT JAPANESE

Back In the mid-sixties, I was a resident in surgery when I discovered that there was a beautiful tradition in celebrating the New Year, that is dropping the lighted crystal ball in mid-Manhattan, to the cheers of hundred thousands of New Yorkers and visitors from around the world.

There would be a celebration in the roof garden of the hospital, dancing, eating and then either holding hands, or just standing together. But most would gather their love ones and take the elevators down the fifty first street and mix with the crowd of milling thousands of people moving ever so slowly to 42nd street and Broadway. In anticipation of the crystal ball falling down and ushering the new year and perhaps to belt few lines of "Old Lang Sine"

On New Years Eve as a welcoming resident I look around for new resident, He was Japanese fellow, thin, and tall with little working English. I introduced myself to him telling him about the blood rush that comes with watching the ball falling down and holding hands singing Old Lang Sine. He thanked profusely, bowing several times.

But he said "I will not go"

I went to the chief resident who went to persuade him that it is an insult if he does not go down with her. She was with williwaw figure, slightly taller than the Japanese fellow; she was noted not to accept a "No" for an answer. Little while later, I saw the Japanese fellow walking as if he is sandwiched between the chief of residents and another husky guy from Israel, who happened to be senior resident. Then I lost track of the trio.

The next morning I was called by the chief resident to rush and assist a surgical case.

I told her "Is this the case where the Japanese guy supposed to help with?"

"He was shot with a bullet in the chest yesterday and today is his flight back to Japan" she said.

OPUS 5: THE POOR BOY FROM SKOKIE (21)

When I was recently hospitalized, I needed the on call physician to check my heart and declare me fit to be discharged.

The physician that walked in said to me "Doctor, do you remember me?"

I had to scratch my memory. I briefly remembered my early days at the medical school. There was a pressure from the AMA (22) and the Graduate Medical Education Committee (23) to appoint other than school bred physicians in a position in the governance of the school. Otherwise the schools will lose its accreditation, so the school in its wisdom and reviewing the back grounds of recently appointed faculty. They found two candidates who fit the criteria suggested by the accrediting agencies. The first candidate was one of German descent, who spent his youth in Germany as a chairman for the department of surgery and me as the second candidate, who was trained in Baghdad, Iraq.

As I warmed the chair, I saw a memo from the dean appointing me as a chair of the admissions committee.

In Skokie, which has billed itself as the largest village in Illinois (24), was largely settled by a German population and later on by a large population of Jewish faith. Currently the population is more diverse; it was natural that a large percent of applicants to the medical school were of the Jewish faith. Going back to the history of the school it was started in the last decades of the nineteenth century, there was an inclination Jewish student into the schools of medicine. One of the wise men in the Chicago Jewish Community started what was billed as a journey man medical school. That meant that most of the instruction was done at night, as students had to work during the day for sustenance for them and to pay the high tuition of medical school. There was general withdrawal of licensing of all medical schools that were not classified as "A".

The only exception was the medical school which was a "C" school, and its leaders at the time promised to make it an "A" school.

This situation lasted until the mid-sixties of the last century when the school management receives it's coveted "A" designation. However there were several caveats that this designation would be summarily withdrawn if certain policies are not changed within the governance of the school.

I remembered the student very clearly. As I was reviewing his file.

He said to me aquiver in his voice "Doctor, May I ask you to be my sponsor?"

"Why do you need a sponsor?" I asked

He answered "I know I am on the paper just like the 300 other students who have applied to the medical school but I know I am different"

"I am a poor boy from Skokie; I have worked since I was seven years old, my mother is a single mom who worked all her life from being a seamstress to become a cardiology technician, and I have four A's that you have taken as the motto for your committee as you see I am able, I am available, I am amiable and I'll be a physician affordable. One I don't have I am not arrogant, Doctor please star my file and one day, I'll make you proud of me"

I did star his file. Few minutes later, the associate dean of students knocked on my door "Why did you star this person's file? Is he from your background?" his voice rising "Is he an Arab?"

I controlled my temper and answered him "No, he is a poor boy from Skokie"

"There are hundreds of people who are also poor" he yelled back at me

I replied "Show me how many poor boys from Skokie you have accepted?" and he was shaking his head as he left my room, and I went to continue the interviews.

I remembered the story while he was checking me. As he finished his exam, he said to me "I told you, I'll make you proud of me. I am the head of the largest cardiology group in the East Suburbs of Chicago and I have kept faith with the four A's and never forgot the fifth "A", then he answered a page and said "My mother says hello"

OPUS 6: THE EXTERNAL EXAMINER

During the final exam at the medical school, before granting the MD degree they had established a tradition of bringing external examiner from the hallowed schools of Britain, France and other countries when they could ask students any questions about any subject. Then the students will either pass or fail to graduate.

Now I did not understand much of the curriculum in Obstetrics and Gynecology, because of the texts that were written in Archaic English. So I decided that I will skip the exam and prepare for the fall makeup exams. At the night before the exam I was relaxing at our local country club (25) enjoying the coolness of the pool and drinking shindig (26). Looking through the magazine that were left behind and it happened that Kennedy's second son Patrick have passed away because of something called Hyaline Membrane Disease (27). The article was written for the general public but it also contained detailed description of the disease, the stages and how the finest most knowledgeable physicians failed to save that baby. The next day, I lumbered towards the medical school and to my surprise the announcer was loudly calling my name as the first student to be presented with the most difficult professor of Obstetrics and Gynecology, I had no choice but to go in. The board of examiners was chaired by several distinguished professors and the external examiner was seated on a big dais and I thought I was finished.

The first thing the Chairman of Department looked at me and said "Oh no not this character again"

As he went and talked to the visiting professor telling him I may not really have the standards of class and he apologized profusely

But the visiting professor said "No, no I would like to examine him"

So he said "Come in young man, now I want you to tell me all you know about Hyaline Membrane Disease"

I couldn't believe my luck and I asked him "Where do you want me to start?"

"Any way you want" he replied

So I started to tell the complex pathology of the disease and its types that could present. I was in the middle of my rattling when the local professor said to the examiner "Sir would you excuse us because we want to ask him a few questions, If you don't mind"

The professor was taking down notes and he said "Sure go ahead"

The local professor proceeds with his question "Where did you learn all of this?"

"Sir when you mentioned Hyaline Membrane disease" I replied

"I was inspired to read all about it", but left out that I read it from a magazine while I was drinking. I ended up with highest grade in OB/GYN in the history of the medical school.

OPUS 7: THE MEDICAL STUDENT WHO COULD NOT BE TAUGHT

I usually had 5-6 class daily on the first year and second year of medical students. Sometimes I would notice a student who despite my repeated explanation who would not catch the signs and symptoms of the disease as I demonstrated by the imaging studies. Now when I started the course in Radiology, I liked to encourage students by pointing out to myself as a student who was always struggling in medical school yet now I became a Chairman as well as a professor while a lot of the wiz kids in the class did not become a professor.

I was telling my students "If there's a will, there will be a way"

Now, the students who are in the classical tradition of Socrates would come up to view the box and try to tell us what's wrong with the patient as he was being tutored by me or one of the other instructors.

There was a student, no matter how I tried to explain to him the findings on the chest radiograph; he would not be able to catch the hint. He was so terrible in getting the guidance that I felt so exacerbate.

I told him "You are hopeless my friend, have you considered going into dermatology or physical medicine and rehab? Where you don't have to look at an X-ray or an image exam"

He smiled broadly and said "I would become a radiologist just like you as you told us in the first lecture, that you do not need to be a whiz kid"

OPUS 8: THE SYRIAN ARAB AIRLINES

Long time ago, while smoking a hookah. I was told this story by a braggart and probably was apocryphal. I remembered this tale when the wife and previous president were being accused of pandering to a certain mid-eastern country for money to finance their projects. It is said that an ambassador from a country, was at that time the dean of ambassadors, a role that he acquired because of the length time he spent in Washington. Soon, after as the new administration was installed, the ambassador felt that he is losing his privileges little by little. He told his listeners that he used to go to the state department, knock on the door but rather kick out and every officer and employee would stand up and wondered why this kind of treatment. He commented that now he has to call the relation desk and get an appointment and asked why this kind of treatment.

He was advised to hire a public relation firm and to keep a low profile until the lobbyist could explore the reasons. The lobbyist came back the next day.

She said to the anxious ambassador "You are a very perceptive person Mr. Ambassador. The new man in the Oval Office told me he hates the Arabs and particularly your people"

"Doesn't the new president realize the cost of bringing Arafat (28) and Rabin (29) to the same table?" the ambassador replied

She chortled "He yelled I hate the Palestinians"

So he said after taking a sip of his coffee "Could you find for me how much money he will accept just to give me the privileged status I had"

The young lady said she will. Next day she came back with a good news, that the next day there would be a celebration in the land of the free and home of the brave for a mere $259 million. The ambassadors ask why that much money, she said to use the money to buy airplane in Seattle. But the ambassador said "We just bought 50 planes from Europe and what will we do with it?"

The president's wife suggested giving away the 50 planes to Syria and uses the money to buy 747 from Seattle.

The president asked the ambassador "Stand up and stand next to me" as he gave a speech at the end of which he said. He accepts the generous gift of the ambassador in the name of the workers in Settle who have suffered from slumping economy.

OPUS 9: THE STUDENT FROM MY HOMETOWN

It was a tradition, as member of the admissions committee, a student will be given an acceptance that has an ethnic origin to a member of the admission committee, provided an equal score on the boards, excellent credentials and letters of recommendations. But somehow, the student doesn't make it because there are several hundred aspiring doctors with the same goal as them and not enough seats remaining to take this student. Now that I am being known to be from Iraq, I was given the Arabic ethnic minorities from the Middle East. A student whose mother came into my office in the Department of Radiology with tears in her eyes basically begging me to have her son accepted in the medical school. Since I did not have any special candidates for that year, I took pity on her tears and decided to mark his folder with a star. It was a sign that I have interviewed the young man he was eligible to enter the freshman class.

After 6 months, the assistant dean of students came to see me in my office and said me "Listen, this particular student that you recommended is about to be kicked out in medical school because he failed all the requirements basics of Chemistry, Anatomy and Biology. I just wanted to tell you as matter of courtesy"

I asked him if I could get a chance to talk to the student to find out why he is failing. After begging him, he agreed to delay the order of expulsion, after I interviewed the student.

I interviewed the student and asked him "Why are you such a stupid entity that you failed all three required classes?

He broke in tears and said "I swear by the grave of my father that all professor were against me because of my ethnicity"

I told him to shut up and sit down; he would be the last student I'll be taking under this quota

He said "What can I do?"

"I want you to bring all your books, come and sit down here in my office every day from 7am until I go home, which was usually about 8pm otherwise I am going to tell the Dean to proceed the expulsion process" I answered

He replied "Okay, I will do that"

And he did that religiously, took the make-up exam which he passed and was allowed to take final exams which he passed with honors.

OPUS 10: THE BUILDING OF THE FIRST MRI (30) IN CHICAGO

The second year after being named, Chairman of the Department of Radiology, I was called by the President of the University. Nobody explained the reason of the meeting as the Dean appeared to be mum about the reason of the meeting. Obviously, I was concerned about the reason for the unexpected invitation. As I entered the office, I was impressed by how luxurious the furniture was. Then the president got out of his chair and led me to a very luxurious chair in his office. The dean was there too as I tried to get from the dean a sign weather this is a good or bad news. As the president said that he has read in the newspapers about a new machine that can image the body as well as the brain with the ability to diagnose Dementia without injecting the patient with any needles or putting contrast in the blood.

I said "Yes, sir I have heard about the machine too"

Then he said "I would like to put my hands on one of these machines"

And I told him "Sir, this is almost an impossible thing for me to do"

He asked "Why? We have all money in the world to buy such a machine and I have heard that you had many good friends who are working in the field. You have 2 months from today to get this machine and prospects of your working with us depends on your ability to get such a machine and I want you to know that money is not a problem"

He turned to the dean and said "We have the space for such a machine and we do have the staff under the current chairman to prove his worth to us"

I told him "Sir, I will try my best to get this machine but remember that we are not University of Chicago (31), Northwestern (32), Loyola (33), Rush (34), or other medical schools who had years of research before us. Yesterday, I had a chance to talk with the representative of General Electric (35) who stopped by and asked him our chances of being put on the list of the schools that are going to get the machines"

He continued saying "Doctor, if I try my best to advance you, I think you would be number 32 in the list of the schools that have already paid for such a machine"

The Chairman and the President of the university told me "I will give you a mission to complete this request by 2 months, to get the machine set up by October and I would like to see you next time and something in your hand"

I decided to throw my hat in the ring. Next day, I took a trip to New York to see a friend of mine who told me that there was a guy who claims who has a machine that uses magnetic rays to image the whole body as well as various parts but nobody has ever seen this machine. I felt I should put him first on my list of people to visit. From New York's airport, I took the cab going to the Fields of Long Island for $100 and got into a bungalow house where the future MRI will be planned.

I started walking between long boxes of materials then I ran into a couple of people who were dressed like physicians. I greeted them and they were indeed physicians from one of the schools in New York. They asked me where I was from and they politely told me that they never heard of our school.

Then I met a chief resident of radiology from Los Angeles whom I felt easier to talk with and asked him "Is the machine for real? Or is it figment of imagination"

He told me "Yes, I think it is real because I had a special projection of my kidney on an IVP (Intravenous

Pyelogram) (36)" and showed me the image by the machine and it was much better than the IVP. I decided to do my own IVP with my kidney which was out of the usual, he couldn't fake the images with a regular IVP which was the inventor of the machine, was accused by his competitors.

So I went to him and said "Doctor, I am authorized to buy from you the first machine. As long as you can deliver it for us by the end of July because the president would like to have it ready by November 1st"

So the inventor of the machine started welcoming me with effusive salutations and invited me for lunch.

I replied "I could not eat because I need to visualize my kidney and as you know those patients are NPO (Nothing per Ora (mouth))"

He said "No, you can have your lunch. It won't affect the exam"

After lunch, I went with him to the machine and slid in to view my kidney. I saw my kidney but better than I have ever seen it before. So I signed the contract with him and left the place to fly back to Chicago.

The very first thing I did the next morning, I saw the President and the Dean and told them that I got the machine for about a million and a quarter dollars and said " I am sorry that I had to close the deal because there were several schools waiting and I was afraid of being listed after them"

The dean replied "Good job, I frankly did not expect that it would be quickly done. Where do we have to put it?"

I answered "I don't know sir but I'm sure we could find a place for it"

Then the President said "There is a big space occupied by the photography department and right under your office"

Talking to the Dean "I am sure we can put that machine there" I excused myself and left.

I forgot all about the machine and the weird professor, inventor of the machine for about a month. Then I received a call from the Dean's office telling me to see him at once.

The Dean said to me "Come out and look at the parking space by the entrance of the basement to the school building"

I went with him and saw piles of steel as he said to me "Do you expect that these pile of steel can take a picture of anything?"

I replied "Yes Sir, I do expect them to take picture"

He said to me in a sarcastic voice "If they don't, I will make you carry these steel pipes" and continued "What kind of engineers do they have?"

I said "Why do you ask sir?"

He replied "Because one of them was asking me about the nearest Radio Shack store"

I answered "The inventor of the machine might be charlatan but I swear to you that the image of my kidney were true"

Now the real issues was installing the MRI unit started because the dean's office was within the magnetic field of the unit that was to be put underneath his office and he did not want to change his office. So we had to get out of original configuration. Within 2 months, the machine was making pictures. I had my brain examined about 40 times and every time I went in feel claustrophobia. The machine was considered an open MRI machine. I asked the students if they wanted their brains to be examined and to my surprise many students are willing to participate. In the meantime, we were correcting the entire device to get a neater picture. One day, I was examining a girl who was in her 2nd year of medical school and I was trying to tell her the structure of the brain that I saw a white patch on the cross section of the brain.

She jumped up and said "What is it, Doctor?"

I didn't have an answer for her and thorough examination by several neurologists. They did not find any sign of disease that correlates with the white patch in the brain. She finished the medical school with flying colors but we could never tell anything wrong with her brain.

The President of the medical school kept a tag on the progress of the work and he asked me "I do have a meeting with the Alumni of the medical school. Do you think you might be able to take a brain scan for a few of them?"

I said "Sure, no problem"

When the alumni and previous students of medical school whom convened, the Chairman of the Board apparently was telling them about our new machine. He set up a desk by the MRI unit and then every alumnus went through the MRI, alphabetically. The President would hold up the image of the MRI and would say "Look how brilliant you are! How much would you like to contribute to our school?" There were about 300-500 alumni present. By the end of the day, we were the first University in Chicago to have an MRI that clinically works.

I asked the Dean "How much did the Chairman collect from the alumni?"

"Over 3 million dollars" he respond "How much did we pay for the machine?" he asked

"About eight hundred thousand dollars" I answered

OPUS 11: TRIP TO ISRAEL

I was sitting in my office going over my mail a little publication across my desk was an invitation to present papers in a conference in Israel. The subject of the conference was about how Israel would survive the increasing expenses of providing medical care to all the residents of Israel with its expanding population. The way I understood it, Israeli General Medical Insurance was based on contributions from labor union known as Histadrut (37). It was mainly made up of Ashkenazi Jews (38) from Eastern Europe. Now that there were Falasha Jews (39) from Ethiopia (40) and other Jews from the Middle East, the Kupat Holim Clalit (41) are the depository of all the contribution of the Israelis in which the expenses can be provided. However, due to different habits from the Falasha Jews and the Middle Easters, Kapot Hapoalim was about to go bankrupt and a new system was sound enable to meet all the expenses of all the subscriber in Israel. I had a few thoughts being the Chief of Radiology at one of the bigger hospital of VA system. I scribbled my thoughts on a piece of paper and mailed it to the conference committee that solicited papers.

I forgot all about the meeting, I did not expect my papers to be accepted for presentation at the meeting. Several months later, I got a very nice letter from the Chairman of the publications and asking me if I would be able to come to Israel for the meeting. I had some money left in my budget for travel so I decided to go. I bought a ticket on KLM Royal Dutch Arline (42). On the way to Israel, I was having second thoughts about my reception in Israel since I am still an Iraqi citizen and my country was at war with Israel. When I landed at Ben Gourion Airport (43), all of my worries dissipated from the warm welcome of the Israeli personnel and I took a taxi to King David Hotel. Next Morning, I was sitting down at the conference. I heard my name being called to go back of the conference room and meet a doctor.

The doctor was a gentleman in his late 60's who said to me "Hello my friend. Are you from the Hindu family that I knew from when I was in Baghdad studying medicine?"

I said to him "Yes, Sir. I am"

He invited me to his house for tea and some dates filled cookies just like in the Iraqi style. The next day I decided to go to Haifa (44) to meet a group of

Israeli Arab Doctors. The meeting was arranged by a group of Palestinian doctors who were in Chicago. So as I was leaving the Holiday Inn, I approached the concierge at the hotel to arrange a ride for me which he did.

As I was waiting for the taxi, another taxi stopped by as the driver called out to me "Are you a son of an Arab?"

I replied "Yes"

He asked "Why don't you come and ride with me"

I answered "No am sorry but I am waiting for another taxi who I have already prearranged"

The taxi driver got mad and yelled at me about how Arabs don't help each other. At that point, the concierge came up and told him "Why don't you take the Shekel the doctor gave you" as he continued talking to the driver "Are you going to get lost or do you want me to take you to jail?"

The taxi driver left and the concierge looked at my badge and he said to me "How's Michael Jordan?" seeing that I am from Chicago.

I replied "I think he is very well"

He said to me "Where are you from?"

"I am from Iraq" I replied

He quoted "Welcome to Israel, my parents are from Iraq too"

As I was chatting with concierge, the prearranged taxi came and said goodbye to the concierge. As I was driving towards Haifa, I marveled at how small Israel was in dimensions.

He asked me "Where are you from?"

"I'm from Iraq" I replied

He stopped his car on the side of the road and said to me "I swear to god that the moment you rode in my cab, you smelled like an Iraqi and you have the sweet smell of Saddam"

I told him "I don't like Saddam Hussein (45)"

The man was so enthused by my presence that he said "I will show you all of Israel, from the south to north"

The first place we visited was a town called Ramallah (46) and then he took me through the highway to see Jaffa (47), as he was driving, he told me a story about Saddam and the Jewish people. He said that the Jews from Iraq believed in the legend that Saddam would not hurt any Jews from Iraq and apparently the word was spread in town. There are a lot of other Jews from other ethnic minorities who believed this legend. All of them stayed in the football stadium at Jaffa when Saddam was firing ballistic missiles into the Jewish states. The first three missiles hit the Yafa stadium and he started showing me and describing with delight, the panic and injuries that affected the people in the stadium. After the short drive through Old Jaffa, we started our way to Tel Aviv (48).

At the main thoroughfare of the city of Tel Aviv, he stopped in the middle of the street, he yelled across the street "Hello friends! I have with me an Iraqi who is friend of Saddam"

I saw two Jordanian soldiers coming to our side of the street and they greeted me warmly. This was embarrassing for me because I really hated Saddam and all of his actions. After a short time, we continued our trip towards Haifa and we found the house of the doctor who was chosen by his Israeli colleagues as the best guy to lead an amalgamation of the Israeli Arabs sector with the Falashas sector and the newly emerging Palestinian authority under Yasser Arafat (49). I understood that the idea was formulated by Mr. Rabin.

After salutations and welcome greetings by the host, he took me to the side and told me in a hushed voice that he could not get more than the three physicians in the room and tried to get all the physicians at the galilee region to come at the meeting but he could not. I asked why

"Nobody trust Arafat" he answered

"Aren't you glad that now you have your own government for the people" I replied

"What governments are you talking about? They are all thieves we are happy in Israel" he said to me

This was a disappointment for me to hear and I decided to return home. After a week back in Chicago, Rabin was assassinated by an Iraqi Jew and the ideas were thrown out just like a rope in the sand.

OPUS 12: ON THE LAKE SHORE
OF OKONOMOWOC

On a rare occasion my son's father-in-law invited us
to share an afternoon it was surprised to find a Jesuit
priest to join us. As the discussions included local
politics, color of the neighbor's hair and how mean
his neighbors were to each other besides attending
the opera, etc. of course the discussion comes to Iraq
and the hapless President George W. Bush (50). I was
surprised by the ferocity of the Jesuit against the
president, as the host knew very well of my liking of
George. After coughing, he mentioned the Jesuit that
my daughter's father-in-law is an Iraqi and may have
slightly different views of those that were expressed.
The Jesuit loosened his collar; he asks me what you
think about George Bush. After recently being in Iraq,
I felt as a person and an intellectual his great wisdom
of his policy. Who made it possible for the Iraqi's for
the very first time in the history to elect a parliament
brandishing in the streets blue color fingers as a sign

of their participation in the election. I started with a low voice saying as an Iraqi, I felt very grateful to President George that every Iraqi should have a statue of him in there houses. After stating my opinion, he poured a drink, as he was drinking it. I was imagining in my head and verbalize; fifty years from now, every Iraqi will have a statue of George Bush in their house. As the Jesuit raises his glass in the air he said "God I am glad I will not be here to witness that" then he left.

OPUS 13: MY FUTILE ATTEMPT

As I was walking to the cafeteria, I noticed a small amount of students than usual. I was told that most of the students were demonstrating outside the school against the government. One of the students said hey you know your girlfriend is sitting in the library. I was surprised to hear my paramour did not join the demonstration, as she was always the leader and the voice.

My friend was teasing me, that love overcomes political differences. I went to the library and it was almost empty. I could see her red hair as I pretended to be looking for a place to read and slowly moved next to her.

"Good morning comrade" I greeted

She said good morning in very curt manner.

"I'm glad that you're seeing the light with these demonstrations outside are no good and don't lead anywhere and that you sat down next to me" I said

She stared at me and slams her anatomy book saying "Listen if you think I did not go out with the demonstrations because of you or anyone else, you are dead wrong. Today is only different because I forgot my walking shoes, I am wearing high heels" as she slammed the book and walk away.

OPUS 14: THE SWITCH AND THE SNITCH

After the Jesuit in charge finished the prayer he turned facing the class and said I want you to take the exam in math with no if's, but's or any other complaint. And that will be the final exam of the semester. This particular Jesuit was known for his idiosyncrasies but was tolerated by the management of the school for his other skills included archery and refereeing baseball games. I was stunned when I saw the exams. I looked around and all the students seemed to be working hard at the exam. A friend of mine was sitting next to my desk. The Jesuit announced there will be five minutes left before pencils down. I whispered to my friend if he could at least help me with some of the questions. He gave me a pitiful look with a slight smile, and then the Jesuit announced two more minutes to end the exam. So in desperation, I took his answer sheet and gave him mine. He was astounded at my maneuver but he started getting down the answers. The Jesuit came where I was sitting and said all pencils down and I

mean it. I had no choice but to give him Jamal's paper
and Jamal gave him my paper. A week later I was
walking by the classroom, when he was an unusual
tirade wanted me to come to the Jesuit in charge in the
class, to tell him what happened. It appears that I got a
perfect score on the exam and Jamal got C minus and I
had to plead with him to tell him about what happened
or else will be flunked. Every now and then when we
had reunions the story would come up. Despite the
fact he became very successful business man. My two
daughters were at a funeral where a colleague of ours
told me that he corralled them and told them about the
incident which is at least sixty year old.

OPUS 15: JESUIT PUNISHMENT
AS A PREDICTOR

I was serving at Baghdad College Boarding school (51) as a prefect for the boarding house. The job was well paying and I had my own room. And it did not conflict with my other career plans. I was enrolled at the Royal College of Medicine from Baghdad University (52). Only 2 years before taking the assignment, students did not accord me the respect or listen to my orders but as the days passed I attained the attention and respect form them. Now there is one student who is a son of a big tribal chief, who is always accompanied with fully armed body guards. One day I saw him harass another student so I gave him punishment which meant that he's not going to participate in any activities for that weekend. He came to me asking to delay his punishment until he goes downtown with his guards. I told him, no uncertain terms and that his punishment was doubled. He threatened me that he will go over my head to the principal. The principal came to see me and after exchanging some niceties, he pleaded the case of the student.

I told him "Reverend Father, here are the keys to my room. Let it be known that s Jesuit trainee did not buckle under any threat coming from a guy who probably be dead if his inclinations are questioned"

The student went to several teachers and they all spoke to me individually and collectively as my stubborn nature prevailed. The student's father withdrew him from Baghdad College High School (53). Years later I ran into a cousin of his at the Medical School, were chatting as his cousin told me that his father regrets that he didn't take my advice and his cousin was found riddled with bullets.

OPUS 16: THE STUDY PERIOD ASSIGNMENT

The first job I got was at Baghdad College after entering the medical school. The pay was good. The time was perfect as it dovetailed with my last lecture in the medical school. As I schlepped my books I rushed to my assignment. In my previous high school, I found out that it is to substitute no one of the other Jesuit supervising the study period. Now the study period is a class time when students sit down and basically do their homework, read or basically anything they want without making too much noise. The study period assigned to me was the graduating class. It was the last period of the day, as I closed the classroom the students started moving towards the desks on the floor making zigzag noises. I notice the others did not stand up when I started the Hail Mary signifying that this is the beginning of the period. One thing that disturbed me, I saw my own brother telling everybody what a joke it is that I would be the teacher in charge in the study period. Getting frustrated at the mayhem that was challenging me I took my anatomy text and banged the table. Everybody was quite for a minute then I told them that I am going to stay until they are quite in the class and nobody is going home until I prove to them doing so. I told them I'm not going to look at who's doing what, I'll sit down at my desk and read my book. The first row will take out their book called appreciation of English and turn to page 300, where Evangeline and started copying by longhand pages 300 to 310. Then I said if I hear one more noise or a desk screech the second row will do the same and the again if I hear one more sound I will have the third row do the same.

Then there was silence in the room and I said "Can we start the class now? In the name of the father.."

I heard the door open slightly and Father Sullivan the principal said "Mr. Hindo is there a problem?"

"No, father. Thank you"

OPUS 17: CRIME AND PUNISHMENT

When I was in my second year in medical school, my family moved to a new neighborhood. Our next door neighbor was a deputy commander of the Airforce. For all their outlooks they seemed to be a well behaved family. Then the revolution happened and things were helter skelter in Baghdad. One afternoon I received a phone call from my mother, pleading because our house help was in prison based on the accusation of our neighbor who becomes Chief of Airforce under the revolution. I hurried home to hear the story and see if I could plead with the Chief who I've done many favors in the past. I waited couple of hours until I saw the caravan of the Chief that stopped by the door of his house.

So when he disembarked, I went to him and saluted as I said "Congratulations on your new post"

And he rudely said hi and went in without asking me what I wanted. So I called him back saying "I need to talk to you"

"About what?" He replied

"About our poor servant from the north who doesn't speak Arabic" I answered

He said "he will rot in jail until he returns the mattress he stole from us". He came towards me with his stick as I grabbed it and hit him with it. His hat fly on the ground as my mother and all the women in the street started crying "Oh, my boy"

I started to hit him in the head and all it fell to the ground and the Chief said you will go to jail. Then police came and took me straight to the Director of the Police in the Capitol. I was surprised they took me courteously.

I was more shocked by the nice treatment of the Police, my own miserable situation for hitting the Commander of Air-Force. The Deputy Commander of the police asked me if I should apologize and told him "Over my dead body"

I saw the Deputy of the President of the republic who I knew very well, that I transported him from Baghdad over the years, came in and told the Director that the President wishes that both party apologies to each other, and I said he goes first.

"You're the one who hit me" the Chief quoted

"You're the one who gave the false accusation to my family servant" I answered

They brought the servant out and said "Sir I did not steal your mattress" After hearing the side of the servant. The Chief and I shake hands and he agrees to release our servant.

OPUS 18: HOW WE FOUND OUT,
OUR BOY WAS NOT GAY

Brian (54) was a good boy but he has a habit unlike our girls who grown up and left the house but still manage to have dinner with us unlike our boy Brian. His mom would wonder what we did wrong because Brian would not say a word about what's going on. I told my wife, give him some time, his still young, little shy kind of boy and he doesn't want to talk about it. We have to give him his privacy and she murmur "Okay we'll see"

"Give him a chance he might have a girlfriend" I said

Brian went to U PENN (55) and then she keeps saying "How come he's in college and he doesn't have a girlfriend"

One day a girl named K called the house and asking for Brian. K was Brian High school friend. She called hoping to talk to our son, catching up and maybe ask him for dinner. My wife told her she will let Brian know she calls. One day we came from the church my wife keep on saying in Arabic language "Tell Brian, K called" repeatedly. Brian asked are you talking about me. And I answered yes.

Getting frustrated I stopped the car and park on the side of the road and looked at Brian and said "K called the house and she wants to invite you for dinner" after I finish my sentence my wife flip and face Brian stating "K is a nice girl, she came from a nice family and she is a good wife material. You should go out with her"

My son smiled and said "I don't think "M", my girlfriend would like that".

"Is "M" a boy or a girl?" I questioned

We continue driving home; my wife is still not convinced on what she heard. We arrived home and as I saw Brian at the living room, I asked him "Can I see your wallet son?"

"Why?" Brian said "Do you have a picture of "M"? I want to see it" I answered

He handed me his wallet and saw the picture of "M". My wife still not believed that "M" is real. She thinks our son is making it up so we won't think his gay so I decided to talk to Brian saying, he should invite "M" for thanksgiving.

Thanksgiving came, then on our door we saw the girl in the picture, I felt relive after seeing her. "M" is an only child of the family from Long Island. We have this costume that there should be only one Queen in the house, Brian took "M" to his room and stayed there. My wife felt disrespected for the reason they didn't join us for breakfast, lunch and dinner. After few days of staying with us, she went home and in my surprise I saw an email with jumping and dancing frogs from"

"M" saying

"Dear Dr. Hindo

Thank you for your kind hospitality. I will try my best to take care of your son.

P.S say hello for me to Mrs.Hindo.

XOXO,
"M"

My wife saw the email and almost broke the computer monitor, for the reason email wasn't address for the both of us.

OPUS 19: MY DAUGHTER HEATHER

Heather (56) is the love of my life since youngest from my girls. She was always curious about life, have her own world of dolls that she communicates with and it was rather content with her own existence. So now as Heather becomes a beautiful teenager and grownup to be an eligible young lady. I was able to fend off a suitor with the excuse that she is still very young to be married. There was one lady a distant relative of ours who was enamored by Heather and she came to me asking for the hand of Heather in marriage to her young son who was political involved.

"My daughter is American through and through and would not like to have a brokered marriage" I respond

I gave her Heather's phone number so her son may call my daughter directly and hope for the best. I went home and talked to Heather about giving her number to our distant relative.

"Why does he have to ask his mother to get my number?" She said.

The day goes by, the young boy is trying to call Heather, but she keeps ignoring his phone calls. I attended a party and accidentally bump into this young man, he asked me to help him pursue my daughter. But I ended up saying to him that I have no control of my daughter, that Heather has her own mind to decide for herself that could I could not help him. After graduating from medical school, Heather decided to go to Africa for a medical mission. After two long years Heather return to Chicago and brought us a lot of story she experiences in Africa. Being home made her decide to move to Los Angeles, California. It breaks our heart to see her go again but we know this will help them grow and mature. Once in a while she will visit me and I will ask the same question all over again.

"Heather you're not getting younger anymore, when are you planning to have a boyfriend? When are you going to get married? Do you want to be alone for the rest of your life?"

And I will hear the same answer "I found someone who will stay with me, cuddle me in my bed and won't leave me. I have my dog"

OPUS 20: DELIVERING MY OWN BABY

At Yonkers General there was a policy that women in a labor be anesthetized in an open method. It simply meant that they can of ether be opened and then put the mask over the patient face and titrate the amount of ether that's dropped in the mask according to the pulse rate and condition of the patient. I'm sure that this primitive method of putting the patient to sleep is no longer the standard or even used in any obstetric delivery room. Now it happened that my wife was pregnant with are second child and she told me that she's feeling the pang of pain. The night before the new resident's wife, who was Italian went to labor. She was yelling "Basta! Basta!" all evening until the delivery. One morning I told my wife that she is going to embarrass us with screams and I will put her to sleep. I was called to the delivery room and I was only the resident available to give anesthesia. So I went to the room and I exchanged some pleasantly with the obstetrician who was from my home country. After my wife was in the stirrups she began feeling the pain earnest.

"Should I start the anesthesia?" I asked the doctor. He nodded his head and said "Go ahead"

I opened the can and put mask over my wife's head and poured about 20 drops right away to the mask and suddenly the doctor said "What happened? There's no more scream, stop giving her more"

Then this beautiful baby was delivered and the doctor was saying "I'm sorry, I'm sorry, I'm sorry"

"Why are you saying sorry?" I asked

"It's a baby girl. And what will I to say to my family?" doctor said

"As far as I know, you don't have anything to do with the sex of the baby"

"What happened? What happened?" my wife asked

"You get your second girl" I answered

EPILOGUE

I came out of Iraq at the end of the Renaissance period which showed the greatest promise of revitalization of the Arab and Islamic worlds especially Iraq. This era began in 1920 with the British expedition which tried to still in the country, the basic concepts of nationhood, loyalty to the government institutions, the meaning of nationhood, and indeed the notion that Iraq was part of the greatest Arab nation. Iraq was a country that was created by Mr. Churchill (57) and his assistants in the ministry of colonies together with General Maude (58) and Ms. Bell (59). General Maude and Ms. Bell tried to cultivate some Iraqis to be the leaders of the new developed country of Iraq which was composed of the Arabic tribes (60), Kurdish tribes (61), a significant population of Assyrian (62) and Chaldeans (63) and a significant population of Jews. In addition, the numerous people who had different beliefs from any of the major groups like the Yazidis(64) and the Shabakis(65) which presented inhomogeneous groups of people that did not offer a nice medium for the rulers of Iraq to have an easy time in creating the country. There was also a problem with the allies who did not fulfill their promises to the Arabs of the Arabian peninsula who supported the British armies against the Germans notably under the alliance of Colonel Lawrence(66) who cultivated the special ties with Prince Faisal(67) who was to later become the King of Syria this to be deposed after a few months because of the Sykes-Picot Secret Agreement(68) which gave Syria and Lebanon to the French and the lower part of the line to Mr. Picot(69) and Sykes(70) to the English. So the British government suggested that Prince Faisal would become King of Iraq which was favorably received by the Iraqi people.

In Iraq, there were several uprisings by the tribes in the South which were mainly put down by the forces of the government. The tribes in the South were Shiates Arabs (71). Then the Kurdish people rebelled against the government. Then the Assyrians who were well connected to the British and to the League of Nations had a revolution of their own. The Islamic nature of the Arabs became obvious when the revolution of the Assyrians was put down with unusual ferocity and 18,000 Assyrians were massacred in the Village of Semell(72) in Iraq.

However, the government maintained its balance and was incredibly successful in maintaining law and order in the big cities like Baghdad, Mosul (73), and Basra (74). The government of Iraq was form every year with a new Prime Minister. Iraq was under British mandate. However, the Iraqi government convinced the British to declare Iraq as a country with full sovereignty and Iraq was declared an independent country in 1932. In the first year of the Iraqi independence, the army made its first Coup D'états when one of the generals decided he would like the ministry to become under the control of one of his friends. When the minister of defense decided to go out to where the revolution was without any body guards to tell the troops that they should return to the barracks, he was shut down by a group of revolutionary officers. At that time, King Faisal the first was dead and his son Ghazi (75) the first was on thrown because of his hate towards the Christians, especially the Assyrians who revolted against him. He was especially in favor of General Bakr Sidqi(76), the leader of the first revolution. He went along with the demands of the army. In 1941, there was another revolution led by the three coronels and was favoring the Nazis (77) against the British. The British then used their allies, the Assyrians, and routed the Iraqi forces that were approaching the air base called Habbaniyah(78) and restored order to Baghdad and other areas that were in the state of rebellion. In the regent, who fled country, came back and took a more active role in running the country. From 1940 to 1958, we had no more revolutions by the army though there were a couple of violent demonstrations, protesting against the British. Until that, black day in July 14th 1958, when the people all rose at the screaming on the radio announcing the establishment of "Eternal revolution" and declared the King and the crown prince dead killed by a deranged officer when Iraq ragtag unit of the Iraqi army stopped on their way to Jordan and killed the royal family in his entirety.

The revolution in Iraq succeeded in one thing only, when it nationalized the oil industry and Iraq received a significant amount of money from its natural resources. However, the army wasted all of the money into buying old Soviet materials and airplanes. The leader of the revolution basically turned on his comrade and he killed several of his closest friends until a couple of other officers turned against him in despite of his big network of intelligence, he and his henchman were over turned and he was killed on Television. Then second original coconspirator became the president under the guise of unity with Egypt (79) and Syria. This goal was never achieved and he died in a helicopter crash and then his brother who was also a general in the army, became the president.

This situation did not last long because the chief of the palace guards and the chief of intelligence combined with a group of officers and removed the president and government seizes to function. Then this group also vanished outside of the country and led to the emergence of a bloody dictator, Saddam Hussain who ruled Iraq without compassion until he was deposed by the forces of the United States in 2003.

The claim or the opinion that the United States and Mr. George Bush were responsible for the apparent decomposition of Iraq into several states fails to see that the United States of America contributed to the Iraqi person in measure of his dignity that he never experienced before and the Iraqis deep in their hearts feel very loyal to the U.S. and especially Mr. George Bush. However, Mr. Bush was not well served by his appointees who run Iraq according to impressions rather than facts on the ground. Jay Garner (80) was appointed as the General ruler of Iraq. But after 32 days serving as a general, he was removed from the position. People of Iraqi was shocked about the news and heard rumors that he accept a 5 million dollar bribe from Mr. Ahmed Chalabi (81).A personal testimony to me prominent Kurdish leader who scoffed at the rumor saying that his experiences with General Garner did not accept the bribe from anybody. Mr. Paul Bremer (82) was appointed Leader of Iraq. Who unwisely treated the Iraqi politicians like if they were in kindergarten by devising the silly concept of each one of those selected as leaders of the country post American routing of the Iraqi forces for one month period each and then he hurried up to leave the country so they can get royalty on his book and then did the most stupid thing in any conqueror by dissolving the army and the security forces without having a replacement or making them without providing for the daily sustenance which was highly dependent on the money derived from their positions as officers. The next day, they woke up and there was no money to feed their families or themselves. This led to the formation of ISIS (83) and its cruel interpretation of the Muhammed Edicts (84). Most of the officers in the army were recruited by Saddam and they were all almost virtually from the Sunni tribes who hated the Shiites of Iraq.

There is no resolution to the troubles of the Sunnis (85) versus Shiites (86) because their basic disagreement was over a matter of 1,300 years old. The only solution that reasonable people suggested is what Mr. Joe Biden(87) suggested and that is splitting Iraq into three parts, the eastern part of Iraq which is adjacent to Iran becomes a confederation state of people who presumably can live together, the western part of Iraq becomes a Sunni state, and the Kurdish enclave becomes a Kurdish state.

This brief history of the modern Iraq, I tried to dissuade the American public from any guilt feeling they might have towards Iraq and not be sympathetic to the pundits who are in Television and tried to embellish the picture of Islamic doctrine beliefs, something which the Muslims call "With derision as Muslim light"

GLOSSARY

1. Dr. B Boghossian – he was a commander of the first surgical advance unit. He was Armenian and retired the army with the rank of brigadier general. A student of Geneva Treatment of war prisoners. An ardent and strict follower of the Geneva Declaration of the rights of prisoners of war. Unfortunately he died at the age of 60 due to cancer of the liver and was buried on the grounds of St. Joseph Hospital in London, England Circa 1995

2. Kirkour – Armenian name tradition of Grigor.

3. ECFMG – Education Council for Foreign Medical Graduates was established by the AMA to standardize the qualifications of trained foreign doctors before permitting them to work in hospitals in the United States. Its headquarters were established in Philadelphia, USA.

4. Damascus, Syria – the capital of Syria and is positioned to the west of Iraq. It is the only city in the world that has been populated by people from time immemorial until today.

5. Irbil – the capital of the Kurdish people of Iraq and currently become prominent with the American air protection.

6. Jordan – it was established by the British and is located east of Palestine. Is currently ruled by King Abdullah the second.

7. Lebanon & Turkey – Lebanon is a country where there is a significant population of Christians and the only country in the Middle East that had a president who was a Christian. Turkey is a country with parts located in Europe and other parts in Asia. It has minority of Christians but majority of its people are Muslims.

8. Military Attaché - it's usually a moderate higher ranking officers in the Army who's attached to the embassy to gather information about the host country military capabilities.

9. Syrian Arab Airlines – was established in autumn 1946, with two propeller aircraft. Operations began in 1947.

10. Valhalla – a place of honor, glory and happiness in Nordic Mythology.

11. New York – a big Metropolis which was called "Baghdad on the subway" by O.Henry

12. Yonkers, NY: A town north of New York City

13. Country Club: A private restaurant and golf only for members.

14. Detroit: a big metropolitan city in the state of Michigan. It has a large community of Chaldeans and Assyrians.

15. JFK: John F. Kennedy was the 35th president of the United States. He was the first Catholic and the youngest president. He was assassinated on November 22, 1963 in Dallas, Texas.

16. JFK conspiracy: There are many conspiracy so theories surrounding the assassination of John F. Kennedy. However, a formal investigation by the Department of Justice failed to prove conspiracies.

17. The O. Henry: O. Henry was the pen name of William Sydney Porter. He was born September 11, 1862 in Greenboro, North Carolina. He was a short story writer. He wrote "Cabbages and Kings" while he was in Honduras and he coined the term "Banana Republic" and "Baghdad on the subway" describing New York City. He died in poverty with hepatitis and liver cirrhosis secondary to heavy drinking.

18. Chairman of Department of Radiology: it is a professional group that meets once a year to determine the status of the radiology practice in the US.

19. Apple Award: It is an award given to the best teacher I the clinical sciences voted on by the graduating class of the medical school. This prize is considered the best testament to the teacher who gets such award.

20. Ben Casey: A fictional character who plays a role of a very young surgeon and meets challenges. He was played by Vince Edwards in a TV series from 1961 to 1966. Vince Edwards died in 1966.

21. Skokie: Considered "The World's Largest Village" and is located in the state of Illinois originally

inhabited by German immigrants followed by Russian immigrants and Eastern Europeans of the Jewish faith. Currently, it is mixed population of Mexican, Assyrians in addition to the initial population.

22. AMA: The American Medical Association was founded in 1847 to help the doctors in the treatment of patients.

23. Graduate Medical Education Committee: Develop and review policies and the procedures that affect both ACGME-accredited and non-accredited clinical training programs and their trainees (Refer to Wikipedia for information)

24. Illinois: It is the 5th most populous and 25th largest state in terms of land and area.

25. Local Country Club: A private Membership club that usually caters to members and their guests only.

26. Shindig: A mixed beer with sweetener and was made popular by the British and Irish communities in Baghdad, Iraq.

27. Hyaline Membrane Disease: This is called HMD for short and a disease of the newborn especially

those whose mothers are obese or have diabetes and it was sa killer at the time of President Kennedy's second sons birth. The tension that was brought for the treatment of the disease helped developed some treatments as it is now moderately easy to treat.

28. Arafat: He was the Chairman of the Palestine Liberation Organization (PLO), President of the Palestinian National Authority (PNA), and leader of the Fatah political party and former paramilitary group, which he founded in 1959. Originally opposed to Israel's existence, he modified his position in 1988 when he accepted UN Security Council Resolution 242 (Wikipedia)

29. Rabbin:He was the 5th Prime Minister of Israel, serving two terms in office, 1974-1977 and 1992 until his assassination in 1955. Rabin was raised in a labor Zionist household. He learned agriculture in school and excelled as a student (Wikipedia)

30. MRI: Short for Magnetic Resonance Imaging is a technique that uses a magnetic field and radio waves to create detailed images of the organs and the tissues within your body. Most MRI machines are large, tube-shaped magnets. When you lay inside MRI machine, the magnetic field

temporarily realigns hydrogen atoms in your body (Wikipedia)

31. University of Chicago: The University of Chicago is a private Research University in Chicago. The university, established in 1890, consists of the College, various graduate programs, and interdisciplinary committees organized (Wikipedia)

32. Northwestern: a private research university with campuses in Evanston and Chicago in Illinois, United States, as well as Doha, Qatar (Wikipedia)

33. Loyola: A private Catholic university located in Chicago, Illinois. Founded in 1870 by the Jesuits, today Loyola is one of the largest catholic universities in the nation (Wikipedia)

34. Rush: A private university on the West Side of Chicago, Illinois. The university, founded in 1972, is the academic arm of Rush University Medical Center (Wikipedia)

35. General Electric: General Electric is an American multinational conglomerate corporation incorporated in New York, and headquartered in Fairfield, Connecticut (Wikipedia)

36. IVP (Intravenous Pyelogram): an X-Ray test that provides pictures of the kidneys, the bladder, the ureters and the urethra (urinary tract). An IVP can show the size, shape, and position of the urinary tract, and it can evaluate the collecting system inside the kidneys.

37. Histadrut: Established in December 1920 during the British Mandate for Palestine. It became one of the most powerful institutions in Israel. Histadrut enterprise include: Koor Industries Ltd., Solel Boneh, and Kupat Holim Clalit (Wikipedia)

38. Ashkenazi Jews: Are those who originated in Eastern Europe. (Sephardic Jews, by contrast, are from the areas around the Mediterranean Sea, including Portugal, Spain, the Middle East and Northern Africa (Wikipedia)

39. Falasha Jews: An Ethiopian of Jewish faith. The Falasha calls themselves House of Israel (Beta Israel) and claim descent from Menilek I, traditionally the son of the Queen of Sheba (Makeda) and King Solomon (Wikipedia)

40. Ethiopia: In the Horn of Africa, is a rugged, landlocked country split by the Great Rift Valley. With archeological finds dating back more than

3 million years, it's a place of ancient culture. Among its important sites are Lalibela and its 12th-13th century rock-cut Christian churches, and Aksum, the ruins of an ancient city with obelisk, tombs, castles and Our Lady Mary of Zion church (Wikipedia)

41. Kupat Holim Clalit – is the largest of Israel's four state-mandated health service organizations, charged with administering health care services and funding for its members (all citizens must be a member of one of the four providers) (Wikipedia)

42. KLM Royal Dutch Airline – KLM, legally koninklijke Luchtvaart Maatschappij N.V., is the flag carrier airline of the Netherland. KLM is headquarter in Amstelveen, with its hub at nearby Ameterdam Airport Schiphol (Wikipedia)

43. Ben Gourion Airport – Ben Gurion International Airport, or as sometimes referred to, Natbag is the largest international airport of Israel (Wikipedia)

44. Haifa – a northern Israeli port city built in tiers extending from the Mediterranean up the north slope of Mount Carmel. The city's most iconic sites are the immaculately landscaped terraces of the Baha'I Garden and at their heart, the gold-domed

Shrine of the bab. At the foot of the gardens lies the German colony, with shops, galleries and restaurants in 19th century buildings (Wikipedia)

45. Saddam Hussein – was the 5th President of Iraq until April 9, 2003 when he was kicked out by the American Forces. He was tried for mass murder of several Iraqis and he was condemned and hung in Baghdad on December 30, 2006. (Wikipedia)

46. Ramallah – a Palestinian city in the central West Bank located 10 km north of Jerusalem at an average elevation of 880 meters above sea level, adjacent to al-Bireh (Wikipedia)

47. Jaffa – also called Japho or Joppa, is the southern, oldest part of Tel Aviv-Jaffa, an ancient port city in Israel (Wikipedia)

48. Tel Aviv – a city in Israel, the second most populous administered by that country's government after Jerusalem. It was the first capital of Israel (Wikipedia)

49. Yasser Arafat – see number 43

50. George W. Bush – George Walker Bush is an American politician who served as the 43rd president of the United States from 2001 to 2009

and 46th Governor of Texas from 1995 to 2000 (Wikipedia)

51. Baghdad College Boarding School – an elite high school for boys aged 11 to 18 in Baghdad, Iraq. It was initially a Catholic school founded by and operated by American Jesuit from Boston. The 1969 Iraqi government nationalization and expulsion of Jesuit teachers changed the character of the school. It has been compared in the British media to Eton College and is arguably Iraq's most famous secondary school for boy, having produced an Iraqi Prime Minister, a Deputy Prime Minister, a Vice President, two dollar billionaires and a member of the British House of Lords, amongst many other notable alumni (Wikipedia)

52. Baghdad University – formerly known as the Iraqi Royal Medical College, was established in 1927.

53. Baghdad College High School – see number 51

54. Brian – the son of the author

55. Heather – the youngest daughter of the author.

56. Mr. Churchill – (30 November 1874 – 24 January 1965) was a British statesman who was the Prime Minister of the United Kingdom from 1940 to

1945 and again from 1951-1955. Church hill was also an officer in the Bristish Army, a historian, writer (as Winston S. Churchill), and an artist. He won the Nobel Prize in Literature, and was the first person to be made an honorary citizen of the United States. (Wikipedia)

57. General Maude – (24 June 1864 – 18 November 1917) was a British commander, most famous for his efforts in Mesopotamia during World War I and for conquering Baghdad in 1917.(Wikipedia)

58. Ms.Bell – (14 July 1868- 12 July 1926) was an English writer, traveler, political officer, administrator, spy and archaeologist who explored, mapped, and became highly influential to British imperial policy-making due to her knowledge and contacts, built up through extensive travels in Greater Syria, Mesopotamia, Asia Minor, and Arabia. Along with T.E. Lawrence, Bell helped establish the Hashemite dynasties in what is today Jordan as well as in Iraq. She is currently buried in Baghdad. (Wikipedia)

59. Arabic tribes: Most Iraqis identify strongly with a tribe (العشيرة 'ashira). Thirty of the 150 or so identifiable tribes in Iraq are the most influential. Tribes are grouped into federations (qabila). Below

the tribe, there are the clan (الفخذ *fukhdh*), the house (الخمس *beit*) and the extended family (الخمس *khams*). (Wikipedia)

60. Kurdish tribes: The Kurds (Kurdish: کورد *Kurd*) also the Kurdish people (Kurdish: گەلێن کوردی *Gelê Kurdî*) are an ethnic grouphttps://en.wikipedia. org/wiki/Kurds - cite_note-47 in the Middle East, mostly inhabiting a contiguous area spanning adjacent parts of eastern and southeastern Turkey (Northern Kurdistan), western Iran (Eastern or Iranian Kurdistan), northern Iraq (Southern or Iraqi Kurdistan), and northern Syria (Western Kurdistan or Rojava). The Kurds are culturally and linguistically closely related to the Iranian peoples and, as a result, are often themselves classified as an Iranian people. Many Kurds consider themselves descended from the ancient Medes, and even use a calendar dating from 612 B.C., when the Assyrian capital of Nineveh was conquered by the Medes (Medes being another Iranian people). The claimed Median descent is reflected in the words of the Kurdish national anthem: "we are the children of the Medes and Kai Khosrow". The Kurdish languages form a subgroup of the Northwestern Iranian languages. (Wikipedia)

61. Assyrian: Assyrian people, also known as Chaldeans, Syriacs, and Arameans, are a Semitic ethnoreligious group indigenous to the Middle East. (Wikipedia)

62. Chaldean: was a small Semitic nation that emerged between the late 10th and early 9th century BC, surviving until the mid-6th century BC, after which it disappeared as the Chaldean tribes were absorbed into the native population of Babylonia. It was located in the marshy land of the far southeastern corner of Mesopotamia, and briefly came to rule Babylon. (Wikipedia)

63. Yazidis: Ethnically Kurdish religious community or an ethno-religious group indigenous to northern Mesopotamia. Yazidism is an ancient religion that is strictly endogamous. Yazidism is not linked to Zoroastrianism but rather to ancient Mesopotamian religions. (Wikipedia)

64. Shabakis: an ethno-religious group who live mainly in the villages of Ali Rash, Khazna, Yangidja, and Tallara in the Sinjar District of the Nineveh Province in northern Iraq. They speak Shabaki, a Northwestern Iranian language of the Zaza–Gorani group. In addition to the Shabaks, there are three other *ta'ifs*, or sects, which make up

the Bajalan, Dawoody and Zengana groups. About 70 percent of Shabaks are Shi'a (Shabakism) and the rest of the population are Yarsani or Sunni. It has also been suggested that Shabaks are descendants of the Qizilbash army led by Shah Ismail. (Wikipedia)

65. Colonel Lawrence: (16 August 1888 – 19 May 1935) a British archaeologist, military officer, and diplomat. He was renowned for his liaison role during the Sinai and Palestine Campaign and the Arab Revolt against the ruling Ottoman Empire. The breadth and variety of his activities and associations, and his ability to describe them vividly in writing, earned him international fame as Lawrence of Arabia. (Wikipedia)

66. Prince Faisal: (20 May 1885 – 8 September 1933) was King of the Arab Kingdom of Syria or Greater Syria in 1920, and was King of Iraq from 23 August 1921 to 1933. He was a member of the Hashemite dynasty. Faisal tried to diversify his administration by including different ethnic and religious groups in offices. However, Faisal's attempt at pan-Arab nationalism may have contributed to the isolation of certain religious groups. (Wikipedia)

67. Sykes-Picot Secret Agreement: officially known as the Asia Minor Agreement, was a secret agreement between the United Kingdom and France, with the assent of the Russian Empire. The agreement defined their proposed spheres of influence and control in Southwestern Asia. The agreement was based on the premise that the Triple Entente succeed in defeating the Ottoman Empire during World War I. The negotiation of the treaty occurred between November 1915 and March 1916 and was signed on 16 May 1916. The deal was exposed to the public in *Izvestia* and *Pravda* on 23 November 1917 and in the British *Guardian* on November 26, 1917. (Wikipedia)

68. Mr. Picot: François Marie Denis Georges-Picot (Paris, 21 December 1870 – Paris, 20 June 1951) was a French diplomat and lawyer who negotiated the Sykes–Picot Agreement with the English diplomat Sir Mark Sykes between November 1915 and March 1916 before its signing on May 16, 1916. It was a secret deal which proposed that, when the partitioning of the Ottoman Empire began after a then theoretical victory of the Triple Entente, Britain and France, and later Russia and Italy, would divide up the Arab territories between them. (Wikipedia)

69. Mr. Sykes: Sir Tatton Benvenuto Mark Sykes, 6th Baronet (16 March 1879 – 16 February 1919) was an English traveller, Conservative Party politician and diplomatic adviser, particularly with regard to the Middle East at the time of the First World War. He is associated with the Sykes–Picot Agreement, drawn up while the war was in progress, regarding the partitioning of the Ottoman Empire by Britain, France and Russia. (Wikipedia)

70. Shiites Arabs: a branch of Islam which holds that the Islamic prophet Muhammad's proper successor as Caliph was his son-in-law and cousin Ali ibn Abi Talib. Shia Islam primarily contrasts with Sunni Islam, whose adherents believe that Muhammad's trusted aide Abu Bakr was his proper successor. Adherents of Shia Islam are called Shias or the Shi'a as a collective or Shi'I individually. Shia Islam is the second-largest branch of Islam: in 2009, Shia Muslims constituted 10–13% of the world's Muslim population. Twelver Shia(*Ithnā'ashariyyah*) is the largest branch of Shia Islam. In 2012 it was estimated that perhaps 85 percent of Shias were Twelvers. Shia Islam is based on the Quran and the message of the Islamic prophet Muhammad attested in hadith recorded by the Shia, and some books deemed sacred to

the Shia (Nahj al-Balagha). Shia consider Ali to have been divinely appointed as the successor to Muhammad, and as the first Imam. The Shia also extend this "Imami" doctrine to Muhammad's family, the *Ahl al-Bayt* ("the People of the House"), and some individuals among his descendants, known as *Imams*, who they believe possess special spiritual and political authority over the community, infallibility, and other divinely-ordained traits. Although there are myriad Shia subsects, modern Shia Islam has been divided into three main groupings: Twelvers, Ismailis and Zaidis, with Twelver Shia being the largest and most influential group among Shia. (Wikipedia)

71. Village of Simele: Simele is a town located in the Dohuk province of Iraqi Kurdistan. The city is on the main road that connects Iraq to its neighbour Turkey. It is 14 km west of the city of Dohuk. The Simele Massacre was committed by the armed forces of the Kingdom of Iraq during a campaign systematically targeting the Assyrians of northern Iraq in August 1933. The term is used to describe not only the massacre in Simele, but also the killing spree that took place among 63 Assyrian villages in the Dohuk and Mosul districts

that led to the deaths of between 5,000 and 6,000 Assyrians. (Wikipedia)

72. Mosul: a city of normally about two and a half million people in northern Iraq, occupied since 10 June 2014 by the Islamic State of Iraq and the Levant. (Wikipedia)

73. Basra: an Iraqi city located on the Shatt al-Arab between Kuwait and Iran. It had an estimated population of 1.5 million of 2012. (Wikipedia)

74. King Ghazi: (2 May 1912 – 4 April 1939) was the King of the Hashemite Kingdom of Iraq from 1933 to 1939 having been briefly Crown Prince of the Kingdom of Syria in 1920. He was born in Mecca (in present-day Saudi Arabia), the only son of Faisal I, the first King of Iraq. On 4 April 1939, he died by accident or design. But what may be described as a historical 'whodunit' also constitutes the peg on which a broader tale hangs: the story of Iraqi politics in the months and years before and after the king's death. Above all, the intent is to convey some idea of the conditions in which politics have taken place in Iraq and the wider Middle East. This episode offers an opportunity to observe the clash of British and Iraqi versions of historical truth and discover, if

we choose to believe the Iraqi version, an example of how British officials and British or pro-British witnesses and historians have denied fabricated, omitted or diverted attention from the facts. (Wikipedia)

75. General Bakr Sidqi: an Iraqi nationalist and general of Kurdishorigin, but not a Kurdish nationalist, was born 1890 in Kirkuk and assassinated on August 12, 1937, at Mosul. He was the first military personnel to plan and execute a coup d'état in the Middle East. (Wikipedia)

76. Nazis: Under the leadership of Adolf Hitler (1889-1945), the National Socialist German Workers' Party, or Nazi Party, grew into a mass movement and ruled Germany through totalitarian means from 1933 to 1945. (Wikipedia)

77. Habbaniyah: a city in Al-Anbar Province, in central Iraq. A military airfield, RAF Habbaniya, was the site of a battle in 1941, during World War II. Lake Habbaniyah is also nearby. (Wikipedia)

78. Egypt: a country linking northeast Africa with the Middle East, dates to the time of the pharaohs. Millennia-old monuments still sit along the fertile Nile River Valley, including the colossal Pyramids

and Sphinx at Giza and the hieroglyph-lined Karnak Temple and Valley of the Kings tombs in Luxor. The capital, Cairo, is home to Ottoman landmarks such as Muhammad Ali Mosque. (Wikipedia)

79. General Jay Garner: a retired United States Army lieutenant general who was appointed in 2003 as Director of the Office for Reconstruction and Humanitarian Assistance for Iraq following the 2003 invasion of Iraq but was soon replaced by Ambassador Paul Bremer and the ambassador's successor organization to ORHA, the Coalition Provisional Authority. In 2003 Garner was selected to lead the post-war reconstruction efforts in Iraq, along with three deputies, including British Major-General Tim Cross. Garner was regarded as a natural choice by the Bush administration given his earlier similar role in the north. General Garner was to develop and implement plans to assist the Iraqis in developing governance and reconstructing the country once Saddam Hussein was deposed. Following the defeat of the central regime in Baghdad, there was widespread looting, rampaging, and general chaos throughout Iraq. Some of the most important monuments, such as the national museum, were under attack.

Furthermore, the infrastructure of the country was in ruins, ministries were broken into, and government records were destroyed. The situation in Iraq became chaotic and anarchic. The only ministry which was protected by the occupying forces was the oil ministry. In addition, many exiled leaders from Iran and some from the West returned to Iraq. The Bush Administration selected Lieutenant General Jay Garner to lead the Coalition Provisional Authority (an intermediary government) in an attempt to rid Iraq of the chaos and anarchy that consumed the area. Garner's plan was to choose government officials from the former Iraqi regime to help lead the country. Garner began reconstruction efforts in March 2003 with plans aiming for Iraqis to hold elections within 90 days and for the U.S. to quickly pull troops out of the cities to a desert base. Talabani, a member of Jay Garner's staff in Kuwait before the war, was consulted on several occasions to help the U.S. select a liberal Iraqi government; this would be the first liberal government to exist in Iraq. In an interview with *Time* magazine, Garner stated that "as in any totalitarian regime, there were many people who needed to join the Baath Party in order to get ahead in their careers. We don't have a problem with most of them. But we do have a problem with those who were part of the thug mechanism under Saddam. Once the U.S. identifies those in the second group, we will get rid of them." On April 15, 2003, General Garner called a conference in the city of Nasiriyah, where Garner, along with 100 Iraqis, discussed the future of Iraq. Garner called a follow-up meeting on April 28, 2003. 250 Iraqis attended this meeting, and five of these Iraqis were selected by Garner's administration as the core leaders of the new Iraqi government: Masood Barzani was appointed as head of the Kudistan Democratic Party, Jalal Talbani as head of the rival Patriotic Union of Kurdistan, Abdul Aziz Al Hakim was appointed as the leader of the Supreme Assembly for Islamic Revolution in Iraq, Ahmad Chalabi was chosen to represent the Iraqi National Congress and Iyad Allawi was appointed as the leader of the Iraqi National Accord. Garner's selection caused quite a stir amongst many Iraqis. Although many Iraqis were open to the change that Garner and the U.S were bringing to Iraq, others were resentful. Iraqis with a Shi'a background felt underrepresented in Garner's selection for government. Three of the five officials appointed as key members in Iraq's new government were of Sunni background, one official was from a mixed Sunni–Shi'a background, and only one of the officials was of pure Shi'a background. The Shi'a felt left out and underrepresented, considering they comprise over 60% of the Iraqi population. Therefore, this caused a great deal of controversy. Furthermore, many Iraqis felt this new government was not selected in a democratic manner as the U.S had promised. Once the leaders were selected, a plan to hold elections in Iraq, where members would be selected, began on May 6, 2003 and ended on November 14, 2003, when the plan was abandoned. General Garner would be replaced by a new American Ambassador to Iraq, Paul Bremer, who took his role as head of the Coalition Provisional Authority. Following Garner's dismissal, it was planned that an Iraq government would take power in June 2004. Iyad Allawi was designated to lead the Iraqi interim authority. Allawi was a former Baathist of Shiite origin. Allawi had many credentials, including previous work experience with the CIA. When Garner was replaced in his role by Paul Bremer on May 11, 2003, there was quite a bit of speculation as to why he was replaced so abruptly. It has been suggested that Garner was moved aside because he did not agree with the White House about who should decide how to reconstruct Iraq. He wanted early elections—90 days after the fall of <u>Baghdad</u>—and the new government to decide how to run the country and what to do with its assets. Garner said "I don't think [Iraqis] need to go by the U.S. plan, I think that what we need to do is set an Iraqi government that represents the freely elected will of the people. It's their country ... their oil."

80. Mr. Ahmed Chalabi: (October 30, 1944-November 3, 2015) Ahmed Abdel Hadi Chalabi was an Iraqi politician, a founder of the Iraqi National Congress. He was interim Minister of Oil in Iraq in April–May 2005 and December 2005 – January 2006 and Deputy Prime Minister from May 2005 to May 2006. It was rumored that he died through poisoning. (<u>Wikipedia</u>) It was rumored that Mr. Chalabi received a call from someone in the central bank of Iraq that he has 35 Million Dollars sequestered that belongs to his family and the individual in the bank said that he doesn't know what to do with it given the chaos and the looting that was widespread in Baghdad and on the assumption that Mr. Chalabi would become soon the President of Iraq and was asked what the central bank should do with the money and suggested that Chalabi told him "I would send a caravan to take the money" and he did. Now, it

was stated that General Garner hit the roof when he heard about the story, Mr. Chalabi offered General Garner 5 Million Dollars if he lets him keep the money that belongs to his family. General Garner accepted the deal. It is rumored that when the American government heard the story, they quickly dismissed Garner and appointed Paul Bremer as a replacement.

81. Mr. Paul Bremer: Lewis Paul Bremer III is an American diplomat. He is best known for leading the occupational authority of Iraq following the 2003 invasion by the United States. He served in this capacity from May 11, 2003 until June 28, 2004. (Wikipedia)

82. ISIS: often referred to in Arabic speaking countries as Daesh (داعش dāʿish, IPA: [ˈdaːʕiʃ]). This group follows a certain jihadist Islamic fundamentalist, apocalyptic Wahhabidoctrine of Sunni Islam. (Wikipedia)

83. Muhammad Edicts: Died on June 8, 632 AD, Medina, Saudi Arabia. Muḥammad ibn ʿAbdullāh, in short form Muhammad, is considered by Muslims to be the last messenger and prophet sent by God to guide humanity to the right way. (Wikipedia)

84. Sunnis: a denomination of Islam which holds that the Islamic prophet Muhammad's first Caliph was his father-in-law Abu Bakr. **Sunni** Islam primarily contrasts with Shi'a Islam, which holds that Muhammad's son-in-law and cousin Ali ibn Abi Talib, not Abu Bakr, was his first caliph. (Wikipedia)

85. Shiites - The major split in Islam is that between the majority Sunnis and the minority Shiites. The split goes back to events in the 7th century: After Mohammed's death in 632, leadership of the Islamic community passed to Abu Bakr as-Siddiq, one of Mohammed's closest companions.

86. Mr. Joe Biden: an American politician who is the 47th and current Vice President of the United States, jointly elected twice with President Barack Obama, and in office since 2009. (Wikipedia)

Printed in the United States
By Bookmasters